Did Jesus Come

GLYN LEWIS was born in Shropshire. Since 1991, he has worked as a photographic essayist, first in Hong Kong where he photographed the plight of people living on the streets and in crowded bed-space lodges, and later in the UK producing photographic essays on the ministry of Agricultural Chaplains to the farming community, the work of Park Attwood Clinic and the role that therapies play in aiding the healing processes, and on the religious order of the Poor Clares. His essay, *The Gospel, told in photographs and words*, has been exhibited in the cathedrals of Wells, Exeter and Chichester.

Did Jesus Come to Britain?

An investigation into the traditions that Christ visited Cornwall and Somerset

Glyn S. Lewis

CLAIRVIEW

Clairview Books
Hillside House, The Square
Forest Row, East Sussex RH18 5ES

www.clairviewbooks.com

Published by Clairview 2008

Cover by Andrew Morgan Design
Typeset by DP Photosetting, Neath, West Glamorgan
Printed and bound by Cromwell Press Limited, Trowbridge, Wiltshire

For Jenny,
my wife, fellow researcher,
and best friend.

Contents

List of Illustrations

Maps:

Asleep in Somerset

Those who sleep in Somerset
sleep sweet beneath the sod
where, legend says in bygone days
walked Christ, the Son of God,
from Pilton-port to Priddy
over Glastonbury Hill
where the breath of God blew gently —
those who sleep here feel it still.

In Somerset, the summer-land
where I was born and bred.
When I must die, pray let me lie
with the Mendips for my bed
that I may rest in glory
where the feet of Christ once trod
and blowing gently o'er me
I shall feel the breath of God.

Mabs Holland

Introduction

This book is the result of my own research, and the research of others before me, into the evidence, the tradition and the legends that Jesus came to Britain, first as a boy and later as a young man.

William Blake expressed the idea that Jesus might have visited Britain in these immortal words:

And did those feet in ancient times
Walk upon England's mountains green?
And was the Holy Lamb of God
On England's pleasant pastures seen?
And did the countenance divine
Shine forth upon our clouded hills?

These words form part of the first verse of the hymn known as 'Jerusalem' that is sung each year on the last night of the Proms at the Royal Albert Hall in London. The practice began during a great National Concert in the Albert Hall as part of the King George V's Jubilee celebrations. At the close of the concert an additional item, not on the programme, was included by special command of the King: he wished that all present should join in singing Blake's 'Jerusalem' to Sir Hubert Parry's well-known setting.

William Blake was a mystic, and in his poem he was referring to the tradition and legends that say Jesus visited Britain. It is a beautiful idea, but does it have any foundation? If the tradition and the legends have a basis of truth are there proofs to verify them? Or in the absence of clear, reliable written records must we dismiss them as being only tradition and legends? But from where can such proofs or records be obtained? Until the arrival of the British historian Gildas, who lived from AD 516 to 570, there are practically no written records of British history, save for a few scattered scraps of information from Taliesin and the Welsh bards. Julius Caesar, Tacitus and others wrote about Britain, but they viewed our country through Roman eyes. So we have to accept that our knowledge of early British history relies also on legends and traditions and we have to hope that these have arisen at least in part from facts and scrutinize them in our search for the truth.

The legend that Jesus came to Britain is found in the words of the carol, 'I Saw Three Ships'. Classed as 'English Traditional', the carol's authorship is unknown, its words and tune having been handed down from generation to generation. English traditional carols such as 'O Little Town of Bethlehem', 'The First Nowell', 'God Rest You Merry', the 'Sans Day Carol', 'What Child is This?', the 'Sussex Carol' and 'The Holly and the Ivy' are filled with images of the nativity taken from the accounts in the Gospels and found in many of the great English mystery and miracle plays. Other English traditional carols, for example the 'Boar's Head Carol', 'Wassail, Wassail', 'Here We Come A-Wassailing', 'The Twelve Days of Christmas', 'We Wish You a Merry Christmas' and the Welsh traditional carol, 'Deck the Hall', speak of the yule log, the boar's head and the displays of evergreen holly and ivy decorations, all ancient symbols of regeneration, fertility and rebirth which in the course of time became associated with the great Christian festival of Christmas.

The carol, 'I Saw Three Ships' fits into neither of these categories:

I saw three ships come sailing by
    On Christmas Day, on Christmas Day,
I saw three ships come sailing by
    On Christmas Day in the morning.

And what was in those ships all three
    On Christmas Day, on Christmas Day,
And what was in those ships all three
    On Christmas Day in the morning?

Our Saviour Christ and his lady
    On Christmas Day, on Christmas Day,
Our Saviour Christ and his lady
    On Christmas Day in the morning.

Pray, whither sail'd those ships all three
    On Christmas Day, on Christmas Day,

Pray, whither sail'd those ships all three
  On Christmas Day in the morning?

O, they sail'd into Bethlehem
  On Christmas Day, on Christmas Day,
O, they sail'd into Bethlehem
  On Christmas Day in the morning.

And all the bells on earth shall ring
  On Christmas Day, on Christmas Day,
And all the bells on earth shall ring
  On Christmas Day in the morning.

And all the angels in heav'n shall sing
  On Christmas Day, on Christmas Day,
And all the angels in heav'n shall sing
  On Christmas Day in the morning.

And all the souls on earth shall sing
  On Christmas Day, on Christmas Day,
And all the souls on earth shall sing
  On Christmas Day in the morning.

The words of this carol force us to regard the carol as either fanciful or an eyewitness account. For it to have survived in the canon of carols it is unlikely to be fanciful. We are left, therefore, with the prospect of regarding it as an account by someone who actually saw Jesus – not as an infant – arriving by ship and accompanied, on that occasion, by 'his lady', traditionally believed to refer to his mother.

The carol's words, which we take such pleasure in singing to its jolly tune, carry forward the legend. The Bethlehem port into which the ships sailed obviously cannot refer to the landlocked village in Palestine where Jesus was born. There is an inland town of this name in South Wales, but the whereabouts of the port referred to in the carol remains a mystery. What the words of the carol do state clearly is that Jesus came to our shores on board a ship that, in the company of at least two other vessels, had made the hazardous voyage from the eastern Mediterranean.

I cannot agree with people who identify legend or oral tradition as fiction or who aver that truth is confined to facts only when they are attested by several documents of unimpeachable reliability. There is no document other than the Bible to verify that King David ever lived or that tells us of the wanderings and deeds of Jacob, yet we accept them and many others as true historical figures and believe the stories about their lives on the strength of a single piece of writing.

I have found nothing in the Gospel narratives that in any way contradicts the claim that Jesus visited Britain. The argument that there is nothing direct or indirect in the Gospels to support the claim may be countered by saying that there is also very little support for the alternative tradition that Jesus worked for 18 years as a carpenter in Nazareth. On the contrary, the account of his visit to Nazareth during his ministry fits in better with the possibility of a prolonged absence, for he appears in the synagogue there as a comparative stranger. Even if he had made Capernaum or Nazareth his home, there would still have been plenty of time for a visit to Britain if the opportunity was there. We shall see that Joseph of Arimathea, who according to tradition was a tin merchant and the great-uncle of Jesus, provided a convincing opportunity.

Some readers may object that a voyage to Britain, as this legend suggests, would have been impossible for an ordinary Hebrew child or young man. It may seem difficult to us, but the writings of Diodorus Siculus, to take just one example, reveal how accessible western Britain was to the merchants, and the Acts of the Apostles and Paul's Epistles show that travel by land or by sea presented no great difficulty to the apostle and his friends. Jesus certainly travelled widely and rapidly around Judaea during his public ministry, and there is absolutely no reason why he could not have also sailed to Britain. Perhaps the chief thing that stops us accepting this possibility is that we have grown up with an inadequate conceptual model of what Jesus truly was like.

For those who have always regarded the tradition as nothing more than invented legend, devoid of any possibility of truth, I hope they will find that I have collated from varied and authoritative sources unexpected facts that are worthy of consideration. I believe my investigations reveal a stronger basis for the tradition than was previously thought to exist. There is a danger, of course, of bending each new piece of evidence in support of the theory, but I have no desire to deceive the reader into believing everything that seemed to support the tradition that Jesus came to Britain. Where I have given space to evidence based on legends that could fill gaps in the story, I have tried to do so without offending people's sensibilities. I freely admit I did see many of the events and facts that presented themselves to me in the context of Jesus coming to Britain. Isolated occurrences suddenly acquired significance for the direction in which this book flowed. But I have endeavoured to bring together, with discrimination, all I could find, fitting everything intelligently into a historical context.

As I conducted my research, I found that I was not alone in writing about Jesus coming to Britain although, as far as I can ascertain, only Gordon Strachan in his book *Jesus the Master Builder* has dared to broach this subject in recent years. I also discovered that, peculiarly, I am one of a number of men named 'Lewis' writing on the subject. In his book *St. Joseph of Arimathea at Glastonbury*, the Revd Lionel Lewis included a short reference to the legend. In the 1930s, the Revd H.A. Lewis, then vicar of the parish of Talland, which is to the west of Looe in Cornwall, published three booklets: *Christ in Cornwall?*, *The Child Christ at Lammana*, and *Ab Antiquo*, each developing the theme, printed on the frontispiece of *Christ in Cornwall?*, that 'Folks say that Jesus passed by here and blessed these parts'. In 1989 the Revd C.C. Dobson, vicar of St Mary-in-the-Castle, Hastings, published a longer work, *Did our Lord visit Britain, as they say in Cornwall and Somerset?* in which he drew on the writings of the Revd H.A. Lewis. I have added to these sources the results of my own investigations of the tradition that Jesus came to Britain.

So I trust that the reader will lay aside any prejudices and examine the evidence presented in this book, and be open to the possibility that Jesus did visit Britain and give consideration to its implication for our land today. I hope too that the reader will critically examine the sources of my facts: the likelihood of legends having a basis of truth or being falsified by people or monastic communities who were eager for honour and gain in periods which spawned many forgeries; and the results of historical and archaeological research. When all these sources are properly taken into consideration, I believe that the claim that Jesus visited Britain comes through remarkably unscathed. I hope that my book will prove an inspiration to all who seek to follow Christ and who love our country.

1

Joseph of Arimathea

In order to discover if Jesus came to Britain with Joseph of Arimathea, it is first necessary to determine the relationship between them and to establish a reason for their coming to this land. According to the Talmud, the source from which Jewish law is derived, Joseph of Arimathea was an uncle of the Virgin Mary, being a younger brother of her father, and therefore was Jesus' great-uncle.

Joseph was a rich man, and later on we will see that there is evidence that he gained his wealth as an importer of metals. He was not only a merchant, he was also a prominent member of the ruling council, and it was he who went to Pontius Pilate and asked for the body of Jesus after the crucifixion and buried the body in his own private tomb in his garden. Criminals were normally buried outside the city walls of Jerusalem and Jesus had been executed as a criminal for the crime of blasphemy: claiming to be divine as the Son of God. Of all crimes, this was the most serious in the eyes of the Jews and for Joseph to reverence the remains of one thus condemned would in ordinary circumstances risk serious hostility.

But both Roman and Jewish law laid it down as a duty that

the nearest relatives dispose of the dead, irrespective of how they died, and Joseph was able to approach Pilate and claim the body of Jesus because he was a close relative and also, perhaps, an important man. That Friday was no ordinary day and Pilate's temper had been severely frayed. Nevertheless, possibly because he knew him and respected him, Pilate granted Joseph audience and gave his consent for the private burial.

The Greek text of the Gospel of Mark, Chapter 15, verse 43, speaks of Joseph of Arimathea as an 'honourable counsellor' – in other words, a man of high esteem. A similar reference appears in the Gospel of Luke, Chapter 23, verse 50. In the Latin Vulgate version, reference is made to Joseph as 'Decurio'. This was the term used by the Romans to designate an official in charge of metal mines. In Jerome's translation Joseph's official title is given as 'Nobilis Decurio', which would indicate that he might have held a position in the Roman administration as a Minister of Mines.

In order to obtain tin, lead and copper, Joseph would have come to Britain where these valuable metals were being mined at that time. The major portion of the world's tin was mined in Cornwall, smelted into ingots, and exported to the then known world, some perhaps in ships owned by Joseph. Fragments of poems and miners' songs, handed down through the ages, make reference to Joseph and it was customary for men to chant when they worked, 'Joseph was a tin man,' or 'Joseph was in the tin trade.' The Revd Sabine Baring-

Gould (1834–1924), novelist, hymn writer and collector of traditional folk songs, thought this might have originated from 'St Joseph to the tinner's aid,' called out when the tin was flashed or smelted. The words of these miners' songs are now almost forgotten but the song that began 'Joseph was a tin man' possibly continued with 'And the miners loved him well' as the second line, while later in the song reference was made to Joseph coming in a ship.

A Cornish miners' song that has survived goes as follows:

Here come three Josephs, three Josephs are here,
All for to bring 'ee the Luck of the Year;
One he did stand at the Babe's right hand,
One was a lord in Egypt's land,
One was a tinner and sailed the sea.
God keep you merry, say we.

The same practice of invoking St Joseph's aid was also observed by some organ-builders during the process of making the sound pipes. When the molten tin was thrown onto the table on which was stretched a taut linen cloth – a delicate operation – the workman would quietly say, 'Joseph was in the tin trade,' at the crucial point in the operation. Julius Caesar, Diodorus Siculus and Poseidonius all wrote about the tin industry in Cornwall. They explain the paths of transportation, overland and by sea from Britain to the various ports on the Mediterranean and elsewhere in the known world of that time, and it is reasonable to suggest that Joseph of Arimathea was associated with this trade.

Because Joseph, Jesus' earthly father, receives little or no mention in the Gospels from the time when Jesus is twelve, most authorities are of the opinion that the Virgin Mary became widowed while Jesus was still a boy. Under the Roman law at that time, and possibly under the Jewish law also, guardianship of a fatherless son devolved upon an uncle, and since Joseph of Arimathea was an uncle of the Virgin Mary this responsibility for the boy Jesus rested on him. The Gospels contain hints that Jesus had friends or even a relative in Jerusalem. Catherine Emmerich, the Belgian nun who bore the stigmata and who had many visions of the life and passion of Christ, asserted that it was in the house of Joseph of Arimathea that Jesus celebrated the Passover that we know as the Last Supper with his disciples.

2

Jesus: The 'Lost' Years

There is nothing written about Jesus' life in the Bible from the time when he was twelve to when he began his ministry in Palestine at around the age of 30. One would have expected that a man with his personality, particularly after the publicity of his crucifixion, would have been remembered if he had lived in Palestine during those years. People would have talked about him. Stories or legends would have trickled down to us through the centuries. But there are none. This is a mystery: where was he during those lost years?

The evidence in the Gospels seems to point to Jesus having been absent from Palestine before he commenced his ministry there. The Gospels of Mark and of Luke tell of him visiting Nazareth 'where he had been brought up', suggesting that he had not visited Nazareth for some time. These two Gospels recount people saying to one another, 'Is this not the carpenter?' or 'Is this not Joseph's son?' as if they recognized him but that he had changed since they last saw him. The account of Jesus' visit does not fit in well with the idea of a village carpenter who has been away for only a few weeks or months.

Further evidence of Jesus being absent from Palestine for some years is found in the Gospel of Matthew, Chapter 17, verse 24. Jesus is in Capernaum with his disciple Peter. We know from Chapter 4, verse 13, of this Gospel that Jesus had left Nazareth and gone to dwell at Capernaum. But on this occasion Peter is asked whether his master pays the tribute tax.

From Jesus' subsequent remark to Peter, 'From whom do the kings of the earth take custom or tribute? From their own children, or from strangers?' it is clear that it was the stranger's tax that was in question. The custom was like Value Added Tax, levied on goods passing through the town. The tribute was the Roman equivalent of a community charge or poll tax, levied on strangers to the town. It is this tax that later on, in Chapter 22, verse 17, Jesus is questioned on whether it was lawful for the Jews to pay it to Caesar, or not.

It is important to recognize that the question does not relate to the Temple tax that was levied by the rabbis, as some commentators have suggested. Jesus, in the eyes of the law, was liable to the Temple tax, and to question whether he was liable would have been an insult and implied a doubt as to his nationality. The question addressed here to Peter implies an uncertainty as to whether the tribute tax was due. It is not addressed to Jesus, suggesting that the tax gatherers knew that he had been domiciled in Capernaum, but that absence for some time could be regarded as making him liable. Jesus' words to Peter might thus be paraphrased as: 'It is only strangers who have to pay this tax. Residents of the town are exempt. However, as I have been absent for some years there are grounds for regarding me as a stranger. Therefore, to avoid giving offence, I will pay the tribute tax for both me and you.'

Jesus, the ship's carpenter?

We can judge from his ministry that Jesus knew about the world and the problems of life – knowledge not gained as a recluse, as some scholars would have us believe. It is the knowledge of a travelled man, and most of the people who travelled in those times were sailors. Anatole Le Braz, in *Au Pays des Pardons*, records the Breton legend that St Anne, the mother of the Virgin Mary, was a 'duchesse' of Cornuaille in Brittany. For Jesus' grandfather to have travelled so far that he married a Breton woman, it is likely that he was a sailor.

Jesus could have trained as a ship's carpenter. Nazareth in Jesus' time was not a very large place and there would have been a limited amount of work for a carpenter. But Nazareth is near the Sea of Galilee and there would have been work on boats. The Gospels record that Jesus left Nazareth and went to dwell in Capernaum, nearer to the sea. This might give a clue to what he was doing during those years – the almost 20 years of his life that are unaccounted for. If he was not in Palestine during all of that time then perhaps he was working as a ship's carpenter on his great-uncle's boats and seeing the then known world.

Evidence in the Bible supports this idea that Jesus had

spent time at sea. In order to rest on long voyages, sailors learn to sleep in the roughest conditions at sea. In the Gospels of Matthew, Mark and Luke, the story is recounted of Jesus being asleep on a boat during a storm. The storm is so violent that the other disciples, some of whom were sailors and experienced in the storms that do arise from time to time on the Sea of Galilee, believed that they were in serious danger of sinking. The Gospels tell how the disciples awaken Jesus, who with a command calms the winds and the waves and then asks the disciples why they had been so afraid. Only one who had been accustomed to sleeping on long voyages at sea during storms and coming through them safely could have slept in such conditions.

So it is reasonable to suggest that Jesus travelled with his great-uncle, Joseph of Arimathea, on several journeys. There are legends confirming this. In Pakistan, where they would deliver tin, there are stories about Jesus having been there; he is mentioned in the Vishnu Parana as having visited the Himalayan kingdom of Nepal. In Cornwall, where Joseph came for tin and copper, there are many stories that tell that Jesus visited Britain, not once but many times, during his late childhood and early manhood. It is said that he loved the miners and spent time and spoke often with them.

3

Cornwall and the Trade in Tin

Cornwall owes its enormous mineral wealth to its geology. Granite uplands stretch from Dartmoor in Devon, through Cornwall to the Isles of Scilly and beyond. Granite is essentially comprised of quartz, feldspar and mica, and when this peninsula was being formed the fluids and gases that circulated through the granite and the surrounding rocks filled the fissures with rich deposits of metalliferous materials. Around the margins of the uplands and the lesser outcrops of granite are rings of rocks known locally as killas and it is here that the richest deposits of ore are found.

The Cornish tin trade can claim great antiquity. For many centuries before the birth of Christ, the Phoenicians traded with Cornwall, which at that time was the principal source of high quality tin. Biblically recorded 'ships of Tarshish', operating mainly from the Phoenician port of Tyre, were the main agents in transporting this valuable metal to different parts of the world. For hundreds of years the Phoenicians jealously guarded the secret from where they obtained their tin. Strabo, who died in AD 25, wrote: 'Anciently, the Phoenicians alone from Gades [modern day Cadiz] engrossed this market, hiding the navigation from all others. When the

Romans followed the course of a vessel that they might discover the situation, the shipmaster wilfully stranded the ship on a shoal, misleading those who were tracking him to the same destruction. Escaping from the shipwreck by means of a fragment of the ship, he was indemnified for his losses out of the public treasury.'

The Phoenicians kept the secret of where they obtained their tin so well that it was not until 450 BC that the elusive tin islands were discovered by the Carthaginian general, Hamilcar (or Hamilco), who sailed through the Straits of Gibraltar and going north discovered Cornwall. The account of Hamilcar is found in the writings of Rufus Festus Avienus, entitled *Ora Maritima*, in which he writes that Hamilcar reported on the tin-producing region there and in his report stated that the Phoenicians of Gades and Carthage were in the habit of sailing the British seas. Hamilcar also referred to 'the hardy folk' of Britain, 'endowed with spirit and no slight industry, busied in all the cares of trade alone'.

Tin is essential for the manufacture of bronze, which in its standard form is a mixture of $95\frac{1}{2}$% copper, 3% tin and $1\frac{1}{2}$% zinc. All these metals are found in Cornwall and the relative scarcity of tin compared to other metals such as copper and iron made Cornwall an important world source. The smelted tin left Cornwall by ship and crossed the Channel to Morlaix, or some adjacent port in Brittany, from where the tin ingots were transported overland by pack animals through Gaul to Massalia (Marseilles) to avoid the dangerous sea-passage

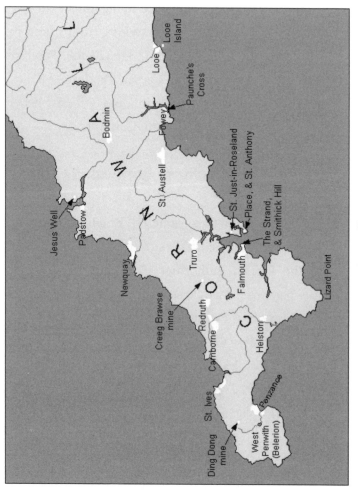

Cornwall

through the Bay of Biscay and the Pillars of Hercules. The trade between Cornwall and the Mediterranean is mentioned in the writings of several Roman and Greek writers. The Greek historian, Herodotus, who lived in the fifth century BC, wrote of the 'islands called the Cassiterides, from where we are said to have our tin'. Aristotle (384–322 BC), Polybius (c. 210–128 BC) and, later, Julius Caesar, Diodorus Siculus, Strabo and Ptolemy all wrote that there was a well-established tin trade with Cornwall by the fourth century BC.

Joseph and Jesus come to Cornwall for tin

When Joseph of Arimathea came to Britain trading for metals, he probably carried letters of introduction from his clients to the Roman authorities in Britain. Such letters would have been useful at Glastonbury for the collection of cargoes of lead, but Cornwall was not Romanized and remained essentially Celtic in character. In Cornwall, Joseph would have had to make his own local trading arrangements with the Celts who lived there, and it is possible that the people in his pay became known locally as 'the Jew's men'. In 1602, Richard Carew wrote that tin streams were first created by the Jews using pickaxes of holm, box and hartshorn. An example of a pick made from hartshorn can be seen today in the Royal Cornwall Museum in Truro. Later, chance finds of tin were commonly referred to as 'Jew's House tin', while Cornish folklore speaks of the 'Knockers' who were said to be the spirits of Jewish miners. One still hears about 'Jews' Houses' (very ancient smelting places for tin), 'Jews' Pieces' (very ancient blocks of tin), and 'Jews' Works' (very ancient stream works) which were also sometimes called Attal Sarazin, or 'the leavings of the Saracens'.

Tin was first obtained from alluvial valley gravels using simple equipment such as picks, shovels and bowls for baling in a process known as streaming. Alluvial tin deposits were the principal source of tin ore throughout prehistoric and medieval Cornwall. Over thousands of years, the tin oxide known as cassiterite had been weathered from outcrops of lodes and washed down into the valleys as beds of sand and gravel. The tinners first shovelled away the overburden to gain access to the tin-bearing gravel. They then used water to wash away the lighter materials, leaving behind the heavier black tin pebbles. These were sorted, concentrated and crushed in preparation for smelting. Tin is smelted from cassiterite at a temperature of about 1100°C, although the metal melts at only 230°C. Smelting was as much an art as a science and depended upon the skill of the smelter who judged from experience when the molten tin was ready for casting into ingots. Thus it was that the aid of Joseph of Arimathea, who later became the patron saint of tin miners, was invoked at this crucial point in the process. A bar of smelted tin crackles when bent, the so-called 'cry of tin' – a sign of its purity. This 'cry of tin' does not occur if any

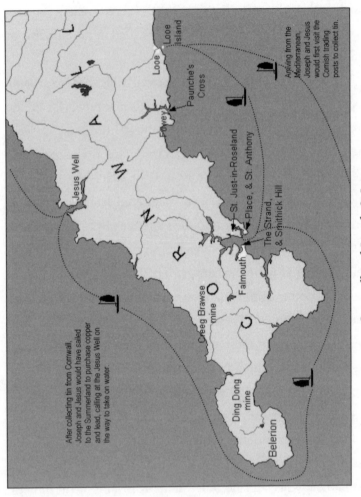

Cornwall and Joseph & Jesus

impurity remains. Cornish tin ingots were generally well over 99% pure.

Legends abound concerning Joseph and Jesus coming to Cornwall for metals. The Revd H.A. Lewis, in his book *Christ in Cornwall?*, quotes a man of about 75 who used to live near the Strand (the oldest part of Falmouth, by the old village of Smithick), saying that his father always used to say that 'Joseph of Arimathea landed at the Strand, crossed the stream, and went up Smithick Hill.' He also quotes a man who was brought up near Chacewater, who said that when he was a boy he often heard the old people say that 'Joseph of Arimathea and the child Christ worked (*sic*) at Creeg Brawse'. This is a very ancient tin mine between Chacewater and St Day. There might also be a connection with Gwennap Pit, the filled-in copper mine and natural amphitheatre that drew John Wesley to use it as an open-air chapel. The Revd Lewis goes on to say that a prominent Falmouth lady, who spent her childhood in Penwith, said that she was always told that Christ visited Ding Dong mine, which is reputed to be one of the oldest tin mines in Cornwall. This mine is believed to have been worked during Roman times, and is not far from the prehistoric stone monuments of Lanyon Quoit, Men-an-Tol and the Nine Maidens stone circle.

In Joseph's time the richest source of surface tin was found in eastern Cornwall and this surface tin was always superior in quality to the later lode-mined tin. Many valleys on Bodmin

Moor show signs of tin streaming and there are several rivers throughout Cornwall that once were navigable but are now silted up, due in part to the tin streaming that took place further up the river. The coastal town of Looe and its offshore island was a natural port for this tin district. The island could be approached fairly easily from Looe Bay and had a good landing place.

As a centre for tin, apart from the tin workings in the Looe valley itself, there was a natural route along the watershed from Doublebois that would connect with the Caradon and Herodsfoot districts and with the old mines at Warleggan. Because eastern Cornwall possessed the richest sources of tin, Looe Island would be high on the list of probabilities of being Joseph and Jesus' first port of call.

Whether or not it can be identified with the great island trading post called Ictis described by Diodorus Siculus and others, or whether there were several trading posts along the coast, Looe Island certainly offered admirably sheltered conditions against prevailing gales. The island's value to shipping as a shelter against the prevailing south-west wind has been noted since local charts were first produced. In the English edition of Wagenaar's *Mariner's Mirrour*, published in 1588, soundings are given for around the island and an anchorage marked on the north-eastern side. The island and anchorage are also marked on seventeenth-century charts (which ignore St Michael's Mount!) and the *Sailing Directory* of 1845 commends the island-lee.

St Michael of Lammana

On 20 January 1934, the Revd H.A. Lewis, vicar of the parish of Talland, which is to the west of Looe, read a paper before Looe Old Cornwall Society entitled 'The Child Christ at Lammana'. He later published a second paper entitled '*Ab Antiquo*'. *The Story of Lammana*. Both papers were published in *The Cornish Times* and copies may be read today in the Cornish Studies Library in Redruth. In these two papers, the Revd Lewis writes that Looe Island was formerly called the Island of St Michael of Lammana, where Lammana probably means a monks' church or settlement. Later, the island became the tiny Priory of Glastonbury and remained so until 1239. This is remarkable considering the connection of Joseph of Arimathea with both Glastonbury and Lammana. There never seems to have been more than two or three monks at Lammana at one time, albeit one had the rank of Prior. This suggests something along the lines of a few hermit cells clustered together on the island because it was regarded as a sacred place. Later, a chapel was built there, while another chapel was built on the mainland opposite.

A reminder of the ancient dignity of the chapel on Lammana is the fact that it never paid a tithe in the usual manner – it was free of tithe. A document of 1727 mentions that the vicars of Talland received a special 'modus' of £3 for the Lammana lands in place of the more orthodox tithe. A deed of about AD 1200 by Hasculfus de Solenny, Lord of Portlo, confirmed the grant of the 'Whole island of S. Michael de Lammana', with all its lands, etc., to Glastonbury, 'which they hold by gift of my predecessors from ancient times' (*ab antiquo*). The document is also important as it is witnessed by '*Helya tunc ejusdem priore*', the first clear reference to Lammana as a priory. The first definite date that can be given for Lammana as being a part of the properties of the Abbey of Glastonbury is 1144, when Pope Lucius issued his 'Privilegium' confirming the Abbey in its possessions. But the word 'predecessors' in Hasculfus' deed, instead of the usual term 'ancestors', suggests a period before and perhaps far before the Norman Conquest. And as the Revd Lewis suggests in his papers, for ancient Glastonbury to treasure and maintain such a small priory so great a distance from the Abbey, Lammana must have been considered very important from a spiritual point of view. That this tiny priory was also venerated locally is shown by the fact that Hasculfus endowed it with the tithes of his domain of Portlo.

The particularly sacred associations of Lammana become even clearer when one examines a curse appended to the deed in which Hasculfus prays that whosoever nullifies the grant may 'have his name blotted out of the Book of Life, and expiate his sin with the traitor Judas'. 'In view of this curse,' wrote the Revd Lewis in his first paper, 'one feels a little anxious about the fate of Richard, King of the Romans,' who in 1239 gave permission to Michael, the Abbot of Glastonbury, to alienate it. The Abbot did so and let the manor of

Lammana out on a perpetual lease and Lammana passed into lay hands.

From that time on the chapel fell into obscurity, and all that remains today are a few stones. The name of the island was first changed to St George's Island and then to Looe Island. But for those who love its story and who regard the site of the chapel as the sacred ground where Jesus walked and sat, perhaps waiting for the commands of his Father, it will always be St Michael of Lammana.

The Father God behind the sun

The Phoenicians were an intensely religious people. Contrary to the mixed Semitic and polytheistic people remaining in the later province of 'Phoenicia' after it had been mostly abandoned by the Phoenicians, the early Phoenicians — properly so-called — were monotheists or worshippers of the One God whom they symbolized by his chief luminary, the sun. The earliest Phoenicians appear to have at first worshipped the sun itself as the visible God. But some millennia before the birth of Abraham, the Phoenicians conceived the idea of God being in heaven and at an early period evolved the idea of the One Universal God as the 'Father God' behind the sun. They further emblematized the sun as the 'Light of the World'.

The presence of a sun-cult in ancient Britain is partly attested by the turning of the face of the dead to the east in burials in the Stone and Bronze Age tombs — the memory of which is preserved by Shakespeare in his play *Cymbeline*. Kymbelin or Cunobelin, Shakespeare's Cymbeline, acceded to the British throne in 22 BC. On his death in AD 7 he was succeeded by his eldest son, Guiderius, who speaks these words in Shakespeare's play:

> We must lay his head to the East!
> My father hath a reason for it.

This exalted religion of the Phoenicians with its lofty aims and belief in a future life with resurrection from the dead was widely prevalent in early Britain down to the Christian era. I suggest that Jesus had knowledge of their religion and of their religious observances and that there is both biblical and legendary evidence to support this, which we will now explore.

Jesus and the Phoenicians

The ancient Phoenician town of Tyre on the Mediterranean was the main port from which ships set out on long voyages to Britain, and Joseph of Arimathea and Jesus possibly sailed from Tyre. During the time when he would have been on ship with the Phoenician sailors, Jesus would have had opportunity to learn about their religion and its practices. In the Gospel of Mark, Chapter 7, beginning at verse 24, a story is told of how Jesus went into the borders of Tyre and Sidon and entered a house there in order to escape from the crowds and the pressures of his ministry. Jesus' peace is disturbed, however, by a Syrophoenician woman who comes to where he is staying and appeals to him to cure her sick daughter. The house was possibly the home of a sailor, perhaps a captain from one of the ships on which Jesus would have sailed during a voyage to Britain, and a home where Jesus knew he would be welcome when he needed somewhere to stay in that region. His reputation among the Phoenicians had probably grown so great that upon his arrival the local woman, who had heard of his power to heal, came and persisted on her sick daughter's behalf.

A further opportunity for Jesus to learn about the Phoenician sun-cult might also have come from the time he spent in Egypt to where his father, Joseph, took Mary his wife and the infant Jesus to escape the persecution of Herod and where they remained until the death of Herod. The traditional place to which the infant Jesus was carried on their flight to Egypt was the great Temple of the Sun at Heliopolis, known as 'The House of the Phoenix', which stood to the north of where Cairo stands today. The Phoenix was the resurrecting sun-bird of both the Phoenicians and the ancient Egyptians – a flame-red bird which after five hundred years built a nest of frankincense and myrrh on the sand and, kindled by the rising sun, burned its life away, but was then to be resurrected and fly down to Heliopolis, the City of the Sun, to greet the morning sun and to be revealed to mankind.

There are elements in this fable that almost make it into a

Phoenician parable concerning the resurrection of Christ, with its resurrecting sun-bird and the golden sun and nest of frankincense and myrrh foretelling the gifts that the Magi – the wise men who visited from the East following the birth of Jesus – would bring when they came to visit the newborn child. Interestingly, it was following the visit of the Magi that the holy family fled to Heliopolis in Egypt to escape the coming persecution of Herod. And there at Heliopolis, to the present day, is 'the Virgin's Tree' and 'the Virgin's Well' where, by the tradition of the Copts, one of the oldest sects of the early Christians, the Virgin and child with Joseph rested and stayed.

The idea of the One Father God was imported into Egypt from Phoenicia and emerged in or shortly before the reign of the Pharaoh Akhenaten. This 'Living God behind the sun', called by Akhenaten 'the Living Aten', was referred to as the Universal Creator, God of Love, and 'Father of the King'. In his pictorial representation he was shown as a sun-disc, each of the sun's rays ending in a hand stretching forth to help man and giving life to the earth. The famous hymn to this 'God of the Sun' by the Pharaoh Akhenaten and recorded in Egyptian writing is a major document of the revolutionary monotheistic faith introduced into Egypt in c. 1350 BC. This new cult paid homage to the sun (Aten), but with it stripped of its mythological accretions. The hymn to Aten speaks of the universality and beneficence of the creating and re-creating sun. Part of this hymn is reproduced here:

Thou settest every man in his place and suppliest his
   needs;
Their tongues and natures are diverse and their skins are
   varied.
All beasts are satisfied with their pasture;
Trees and plants are flourishing,
The birds which fly from their nests stretch out their wings
   in praise to thee;
The fish in the rivers dart before thy face;
Thy rays are in the midst of the great green sea.
Rising as the living Aten – appearing, shining, distant or
   near,
Thou makest millions of forms from thyself alone.
The world came into being by thy hand, according as thou
   hast made them.
When thou hast risen they live; when thou settest they die,
For thou art lifetime itself; one lives through thee.
Eyes are fixed on thy beauty until thou settest.
Thou, living Aten, the beginning of life,
Thou art gracious, great, glist'ning, high above every land.

Written over three centuries before David, this hymn to
Aten is generally regarded as the non-Jewish source of Psalm
104. Jesus, with his knowledge of both the Psalms and the
Phoenician sun-cult, cannot have failed to notice the simila-
rities of thought and shared belief expressed in the two. And
his time spent in Egypt as a child provides an additional

explanation of how Jesus could have gained his knowledge of the religion and the religious exercises of the Phoenicians, some of whom he would have met on visits to Britain with Joseph, trading for tin.

We must also consider the attitude the Phoenicians might have had towards Jesus. Jesus, perhaps, made a great impression upon the sailors with whom he travelled and with those who would have given Joseph and Jesus hospitality at the trading posts. Next, we will learn how the Phoenicians might have provided protection for Jesus and Joseph during the time of their stay on Looe Island, and of an ancient cross attributed to the Phoenicians.

The Giants' Hedge

To the north-west of Looe there is a line known as the Giants' Hedge and marked as such on local maps. The line comprises an earthwork, topped with a hedge. Folklore recounts how the piskies of Cornwall, hearing that a little boy and his uncle had landed at Lammana, hastened to the Giants and convinced them to build the Hedge to protect the vulnerable humans during their stay (*Christ in Cornwall?*, by the Revd H.A. Lewis).

Before we dismiss this as a charming piece of nonsense, we would do well to consider what L.A. Waddell wrote in his book *The Phoenician Origin of Britons, Scots and Anglo-Saxons*. He says that the word 'piskies' is Cornish for the cave-dwelling and earth-burrowing Picts, who were aptly described by Aeschylus in *Prometheus Bound*:

No craft they knew
with woven brick or jointed beam to pile
the sunward porch; but in the dark earth burrowed
and housed, like tiny ants in sunless caves.

If the piskies are Picts, then who are the Giants, the traditional occupiers of Britain before the builders of stone circles, megaliths and 'giants' tombs' in Britain, Brittany and in other places colonized by the Phoenicians? It is significant that the Amorites of Syria-Phoenicia-Palestine are called 'giants' by the Hebrews in the Old Testament. They are, moreover, also called 'the sons of Anak', and 'anak' in Akkadian is a name for tin.

So a reinterpretation of the legend associated with the Giants' Hedge might read:

The Picts, hearing that a little boy and his uncle (Jesus and Joseph) had landed at Lammana, and knowing of the marauders on the mainland around Looe and the threat they posed, asked the Phoenician tinners to erect a defence, which they did in the form known today as the Giants' Hedge.

Paunche's Cross

At the eastern tip of the mouth of the River Fowey is a colony of rocks and on the biggest rock there stands a wooden cross.

It is known as Paunche's Cross and it has held this name for centuries. In 1525 the historian John Leland referred to it by this name. It was still known as Paunche's Cross in the 1940s and today it is sometimes referred to as 'The Jesus Cross'.

The symbol of the cross as a sun cross appears in various forms in most places where the Phoenicians penetrated, and is found widely in India. In the *Mahabharata*, an Indian epic of the Great Barats, the Phoenicians are referred to as 'the able Panch', who set out to invade the earth and 'brought the whole world under their sway'. The name Panch in the Indian epic and the name Paunche given to this cross are incredibly similar.

The Phoenicians venerated the symbol of the cross as the emblem of the universal victory of the One God, symbolized by the sun. The cross was worn on a person for adoration or as an amulet or charm. There were also larger crosses for adoration or for abjuration. These crosses were made of wood. All ancient specimens have now perished but their use in Britain was once quite widespread. The modern super-stition of 'touch wood' in order to avert ill-luck is a survival of the wooden cross being associated with this sun-cult. But neither the cross nor the sun itself, of which the cross was the symbol, were the objects of worship among these early Phoenicians, but the supreme God behind both the cross and the sun.

If the name Paunche was given to the cross near Fowey because one was erected there by the Phoenicians, then it is possible that it dates from the time when Joseph of Arimathea returned to Britain following the crucifixion of Jesus. Landing at St Just-in-Roseland, before journeying to Glastonbury Joseph probably revisited all the places along the south coast where in the past he had traded for metals. He would have told his Phoenician mining and trading friends how Jesus, through his crucifixion on the cross, had brought atonement for wrongs. Some of the Phoenicians might have remembered Jesus coming with Joseph and, endowed with such an exalted religion themselves, it is possible that they embraced the religion of Christ and transferred it to their sacred cross. If so, then it is they who erected the Paunche cross in his memory.

4

The Roseland Peninsula

The early explorer Pytheas of Massalia (352–323 BC) cir-
cumnavigated Britain and first mapped it out scientifically
with latitudes. He visited Belerion (West Penwith, Cornwall)
and the tin-exporting island of Ictis, and he then sailed north
as far as Shetland, surveying and landing at several places on
the way. Diodorus Siculus, writing in the first century BC,
quotes Pytheas' report and writes much about the Cornish tin
trade. He says that the Cornish were friendly and civilized
due to their contact with the Mediterranean traders. He
describes how the people of Belerion prepared the tin, care-
fully working the ground containing 'earthy veins, the pro-
duce of which is ground down, smelted and purified'.
Diodorus said that the smelted tin was beaten into 'four-
square pieces, the size of dice', and then conveyed to a great
trading post on an island known as Ictis, which could only be
approached at low tide, where the ingots were loaded onto
the traders' ships. Some think that the island of Ictis is what
we know today as St Michael's Mount, others that it is Looe
Island, also known as St George's Island or Lammana, or even
as far east as the Isle of Wight.

Ptolemy and others speak of a Valuba or Valubia as a chief

port of Britain and this has been identified by many with the Fal estuary, which is the largest natural harbour in Britain, and the third largest natural harbour in the world (the other two being Sidney and Rio). It is directly opposite Morlaix and a rock off the adjacent coast is sometimes pointed out as being the nearest land to Brittany. It seems unlikely that ships coming across the Channel from Morlaix in Brittany would sail west to St Michael's Mount. Rather, it is more probable that they would have crossed over to the area around the Fal or veered with the prevailing westerly winds eastwards towards Looe.

The Roman historian Pliny the Younger (AD 23–79) also disagrees with the view that Ictis is St Michael's Mount. In those times, he says, St Michael's Mount was part of the mainland and had rocky shores. The old Mediterranean sailors used to beach their boats and they could not have done this there. He describes another island near to where Falmouth is today and this could have been the area around St Anthony on the Roseland peninsula. It is important to note that the word 'island' in the literature of those times was sometimes also applied to peninsulas and to maritime regions. Some writers say that the parish of St Anthony was once an island, with the sea coming up Froe Creek on the right of the road going towards St Anthony and out by Towan beach. There is geological evidence to support this. At Porth there is a narrow neck of land, on the upper part of which lies a sandbank. The bank is at least 30 feet above the high-water mark. This sandbank, with its upper part of siliceous sand

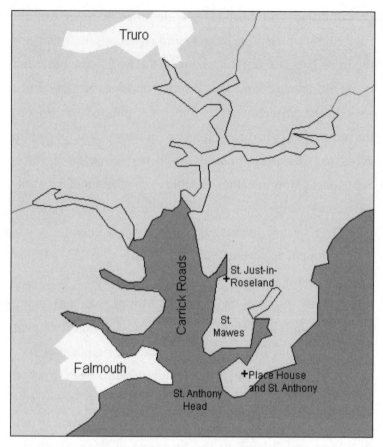

The Fal Estuary and Roseland Peninsula

and the lower part intermixed with pebbles, resembles the banks on the shores of Mount's Bay. Consequently, there would have been much more water in the Creek then than there is today. The Phoenicians could have come in on the tide and beached their boats in the cove. Today, Amsterdam Bay opposite Place on the Roseland Peninsula is still one of the safest coves in Cornwall.

Place

It is thought that the Phoenicians established a trading post at Place in order that they could do business with the Cornish before their merchant ships arrived. An H-shaped ingot of tin weighing 158 pounds, dredged up in St Mawes Harbour in 1820 and today on display in the Royal Cornwall Museum in Truro, may date from Phoenician times and if so would support the theory that Place was a trading post for this metal. In order to have somewhere that they could live in safety the Phoenicians built a fort, here on the Roseland peninsula at almost its most southerly point, where Place House stands today. The Phoenicians did not build with mud and wattle. They used stone, and in later times the Celtic monks probably used this building as their monastery.

But while the Celtic form of religion centred on the monastery, the Roman centred on the parish. In the Catholic system the priest had his parish. He knew his boundaries and his obligations, and there was a bishop over him to see that he did his work properly. There was order and method. In the Celtic system, the monks went forth from the monastery and preached the Gospel wherever their feet took them, just as Christ's disciples did. It was the earliest form of Christianity and it came directly from Palestine and not through Rome. One was an established form of Christianity, the other a missionary one.

Dedicated to St Mary, the Celtic monastery and convent

that existed at Place was said to be one of the first monasteries built in Britain. Celtic monasteries usually had a convent attached. The one at Place was the priory and convent of St Mary-de-Valle and remained so until King Athelstane invaded Cornwall. It was Athelstane's policy to replace the few remaining Celtic monasteries in his day with Roman orders of monks. After his victory over the Cornish at the battle of Valandruth in 933, he marched to Roseland where he turned the Celtic monks out of Place and left a caretaker party of four Augustinian monks to keep the building occupied until his plans were completed. Under his instructions, the priory, convent and church were temporarily put under the jurisdiction of the Abbot and Conclave of Tavistock in Devon.

Athelstane's next step was to order the old Celtic church to be converted into a small cathedral, built in the shape of a cross with a tower in the centre of the building. It is one of the most perfect examples of early Christian church architecture to be found anywhere in Britain. A bishop was appointed and the monastery was called 'Place', an old Saxon word for 'palace'. It became the bishop's palace. Today it is the church of St Anthony-in-Roseland.

St Anthony-in-Roseland

Tucked in behind Place House stands the church of St Anthony-in-Roseland. The church is reached by climbing over a stone stile and following a short wooded footpath leading through the churchyard. Over the south door, at the entrance to the church, is an arch. What is wonderful about the arch is not its age – it has been there for more than 1000 years – nor its beauty, even though it is a very beautiful piece of work. It is the story, said to be told in ancient pictographs between the dog-teeth and the voussoirs, that Jesus visited here with Joseph of Arimathea.

The arch was built on the instruction of King Athelstane in 933. The first Bishop of St Anthony-in-Roseland was a Saxon, probably trained abroad, and it is thought that he was responsible for the design of this wonderful arch over the south door of the church. On the Continent he would have seen Norman architecture and perhaps he admired it. But he was a Saxon so he combined the two forms of architecture in the archway to his cathedral and thus the arch is a combination of the two different forms – Norman and Saxon. There are two arched rows of dog-teeth after the Norman fashion and a Saxon arch inside with the sign of the Lamb and the Cross carved on one of the stones of the Saxon arch. The Lamb and the Cross are not in the centre as there is no keystone to the arch. The arch is supported by Saxon pillars.

The generally held view is that this arch was purchased from the priory of Plympton in Devon and erected when the church was restored in 1851; another view is that it was erected when the church was restored in 1124 by William Warlast, then Saxon Bishop of Exeter. This view may derive its source from the writings of the Cornish historian Charles

Henderson, who wrote at great length on various Cornish churches. Having seen the church of St Anthony with its early English arches and window frames, he decided that it was an early English church. Charles Henderson wrote that the arch was probably bought from Plympton and other writers following him have copied this idea. The outer arch is built of Caen stone from Normandy but the stones that make up the inner Saxon arch are of local origin, probably brought from the greenstone quarry of Pentewan on the coast west of St Austell. Further, the outer arch has the appearance of being pre-Norman and if so pre-dates the priory at Plympton, which was not built until 1121.

Let us return to the story told on the arch that Jesus visited here with Joseph of Arimathea. In the 1970s, a Mr Edward Harte managed Place House as a hotel. Edward Harte wrote a guide and history of Place and the church of St Anthony-in-Roseland, a copy of which may be seen in the Cornish Studies Library in Redruth. In his guide, Edward Harte describes how the series of pictographs carved between the rows of dog-teeth and the voussoirs of the Saxon arch were interpreted by a visiting archaeologist as being esoteric signs. The archaeologist told Edward Harte that he had seen similar pictographs on a doorway leading to an ancient temple at Dendera in Lower Egypt belonging to the later Hyksos dynasties.

The presence of Phoenician pictographs on the doorway to the temple in Lower Egypt may be explained by the long connections of the Phoenicians with the Egyptians. Phoenician ships are found depicted on Egyptian reliefs of the time of Sahure in the fifth dynasty at around 2500 BC, and by the eighteenth century BC there was an extensive trade in timber and artistic commodities between Phoenicia and Egypt. During the fifteenth to seventeenth dynasties, Egypt was under the Hyksos who around 1750 invaded Lower Egypt. The eighteenth and nineteenth dynasties saw the golden age of Egyptian expansion and power, and Phoenicia came under the economic and quasi-military control of Egypt with several Phoenician towns claimed to have been captured by the Pharaoh Tuthmosis III (c. 1485 BC).

In many places in the world where the Phoenicians travelled and traded they brought their forms of writing. They used Ogam for commerce and for the recording of events, but wrote in pictographic symbols when something of special or religious importance needed to be recorded. These symbols sometimes related to the positions of heavenly bodies at the time the event being described took place. The visiting archaeologist interpreted the pictographs on the arch of the south door to the church of St Anthony-in-Roseland as telling of Jesus' birth and of his visit to Place. The Lamb and the Cross face the rising sun, meaning that he was here in his early life – his future was before him. Because it is on the left of the centre line it indicates that he was here just before the turn of the year, probably in December. There are echoes here of the carol 'I Saw Three Ships', with its reference to the ships sailing in on the morning of Christmas Day, obviously in

December. If these interpretations are correct then the pictographs on this arch are a copy of an earlier inscription dating back to the time of the Mediterranean traders at Place, and make this arch one of the few ancient records that exist to support the legend that Jesus visited Britain.

A steeple, within which hangs a single bell, surmounts the tower of the church of St Anthony-in-Roseland. The observant visitor will notice that this bell does not swing, as one would expect in a steeple obviously added for the purpose of installing a bell, but instead is fixed with the bell rope attached to the clapper. The history of this bell and an explanation why the bell does not swing are given in the guide written by Edward Harte and reproduced here:

Until Victorian times, as mentioned in records con-temporary with Edward VI, the church of St. Anthony-in-Roseland had only one bell. In the restoration work carried out in 1851 it was decided that a steeple should be added to the tower and a new bell installed and for this purpose a bell, 12 inches in diameter and cast at Francis Dingey's foundry in Truro, was purchased.

In order to install the steeple, part of the old Saxon tower had to be dismantled. This meant taking the old bell down. As it was not very big, no one thought it would be heavy. It is incredibly heavy, and as soon as the bell was loosed the men could not hold it and it came crashing down, smashing the tiles below to smithereens. But the bell was not cracked or even scratched. To the men of those days this was impossible: they thought it was a miracle. Today you can see the Spry Arms set in the floor where the tiles were broken, to commemorate it. At a later date the bell was examined and found to be made of wroth bronze, a form of bronze that is extremely dense and heavy and that does not corrode.

In Jerusalem, in the Archaeological Museum in the Jordan Quarter, is a collection of articles made of wroth bronze and some of the stone moulds they were made in. The Director of the Museum will tell you that the last people who knew how to make this metal were of Phoenician origin and lived in the middle Bronze Age. If this bell is really made of wroth bronze then the question comes to mind of why the Phoenicians carried a bell of such great weight over a distance of 2,000 miles to Place. On the other hand, the bell might have been made in Cornwall.

Further proof that the bell is made of wroth bronze is found in its state of tune. Bells have to be tuned periodically – approximately every 25 years if they are to keep their note. Examination of the bell in the steeple of St. Anthony-in-Roseland confirms that it is a virgin bell: a bell that has been cast true the first time and has not been touched since. This bell has never been tuned in all the thousands of years of its existence.

We know that the bell was in the church four hundred years ago as it is mentioned in a catalogue of bells contemporary with Edward VI. In the 1850s it fell 80 ft. and smashed the tiles below to pieces. When they re-hung the bell in the new wooden spire they could not swing it. A bell of its weight would tear the spire to pieces, so it was fixed. The clapper has struck the same spot on the bell since then and when the bell is rung its note rings clear and true, sending a river of sound for a full half minute afterwards, with its note not altering half a semitone. There is no other metal on earth but wroth bronze hard enough to keep the bell so true.

And the new bell? Edward Harte says it was hung above the porch in Place House. They did this, he writes,

> ...so that it could be used in an emergency to attract the attention of the Fire Brigade in St. Mawes in case of fire. Incidentally, the bell rope was let into the front porch but was later taken away just after the house was converted into a hotel. So many guests returning late at night had thought it a good idea to pull the rope!

Thus reads Edward Harte's account of the bell in the steeple. The current guide to the church disagrees with Edward Harte's account and says that the original bell was destroyed when the tower fell down in about 1700 and that the bell hanging in the steeple today is the new bell cast by Francis Dingey's foundry. This, however, does not explain why the bell is fixed and does not swing, as would normally be the case where a new steeple has been built for the purpose of housing a new bell. Some writers deny that the Phoenicians ever came to Cornwall. Although they do admit to a trade in tin between Cornwall and 'Mediterranean peoples', they fail to identify who they believe these Mediterranean traders were. But if what Edward Harte wrote is true and it is the old bell that hangs in the steeple today then this provides further substantive evidence that Place was a trading post for the Phoenicians.

And what is wroth bronze? It is almost certain that the Bronze Age peoples experimented with varying percentages of tin and zinc added to copper and so discovered different forms of bronze. Today, for example, we know that gunmetal, comprising approximately 88% copper, 8–10% tin and 2–4% zinc, is used for parts that are subject to wear or to corrosion, especially by sea water. Phosphor bronze, comprising 92–98% copper, 2–8% tin and 0.1–0.4% phosphorous is hard enough to be used in gears, bearings and cylinder cases. But if we have lost the knowledge of how to make wroth bronze or even forgotten what it is, then a quotation by Edward Harte from the Egyptologist Richard H. Wilkinson might prove instructive: 'The use of copper, bronze and other metals was known to the ancient Egyptians before the Exodus, and they appear to have understood the art of both hardening bronze and of making it flexible to a degree unknown to us.'

Before we leave the church of St Anthony-in-Roseland we

must look at a further possible piece of evidence dating from earlier times. In the centre of the east wall of the north transept there is a window that has no proper sill and reaches nearly to the ground. This window was present before the reformation of the church in the 1850s and shows that this north transept, though six feet shorter than the south transept, was so in the original design. This window has been formed to resemble the other windows in the church. On either side of the window there are two ancient door jambs, and the stones on the wall outside reveal the outline of what was once a large doorway. No Christian building would have such a large doorway in an east-facing wall, and since the current guide to the church does not mention this doorway we must presume that it dates from when the Celtic monastery was here, or even earlier to the time of the Phoenician trading post.

Edward Harte records that the right-hand door jamb – the one nearest the piscina in the north transept – has been identified as a panel containing an inscription relating to the story of Jesus' visit to Place. In his guide to Place he writes:

The panel starts with the ancient sign of Icthus – a fish, and a sign used in early Christian times when to be a Christian meant persecution. It comes from the Greek phrase – literally, 'Jesus Christ, God, Son, Saviour'. The first letter of each word spells Icthus, which is the Greek word for a fish.

Below this is found the top portion of a ship with its sails furled, meaning the ship was at anchor. You can then see our Lord's head with the crown of thorns. The inscription is in Ogam, an earlier form of linear writing used by the Celtic monks and found a lot on stones in Ireland. The Phoenicians used it for their accounts and records and the Celts probably learned it from the Phoenicians through their trade with them.

Ogam writing has only 16 characters but it has many permutations. In a way it is like shorthand. The same symbol on the front of the stone has a different meaning when it is on the right side and again when it is on the left side. There is an early method where a rough line is drawn down the centre with the characters on each side. In this inscription both methods are used. The transition from the earlier to the later is why experts say the inscription is so old.

This panel has been examined by many experts, who are all of the opinion that it dates from no later than the end of the first century or the beginning of the second. A rubbing has been taken of the inscription on the panel and it is said to relate the same story about Jesus' visit that is carved on the doorway outside. If this is true, and Jesus indeed stayed here, then this was carved within living memory of the event and was probably copied from the account Joseph and Jesus left behind. Here is documentary proof and not a legend.

Edward Harte is not quite correct in saying that Ogam writing has only 16 characters as there are other forms with a different number of characters. But the Phoenician style of Ogam reserved for subjects of sacred or religious importance was indeed the style that used 16 characters. If the account and description given by Edward Harte are true then this panel is the earliest dated Christian artefact in Cornwall, and the interpretation of its meaning provides further documentary evidence of Jesus having come to our shores. An article in *Cornish Life*, Vol. 17, No. 3, published in March 1990 and written by John Macleay, also mentions this inscribed stone panel being in the church.

At the dissolution of the monasteries, St Anthony-in-Roseland did not acknowledge the authority of the Archbishop of Canterbury, its spiritual jurisdiction being independent of the archdeacon and subject immediately to the bishop at that time. Even when the parish was later amalgamated with the parish of Gerrans for services, the Ecclesiastical Commission was not responsible for the upkeep of the church. This unusual financial independence accords with a similar independence relating to the church on Looe Island, the old St Michael of Lammana, which never paid a tithe and is another special place uniquely connected with Jesus' and Joseph's visit. The church of St Anthony-in-Roseland today is in the care of the Churches Conservation Trust and stands as a testimonial to the truth of our conviction that Christ came to Britain.

1. Ding Dong Mine

2. Looe Island

3. *The Giants' Hedge*

4. *Paunche's Cross*

5. *Place House, the Roseland Peninsula*

6. *The south door, St Anthony-in-Roseland*

7. *The bell, St Anthony-in-Roseland*

8. *St Anthony Head*

9. St Just-in-Roseland

10. Glastonbury Tor from Wearyall Hill
(with the Glastonbury Thorn in the foreground)

11. The Jesus Well, north of the Camel Estuary

12. A reconstruction of a log boat

13. St Joseph's Chapel, Glastonbury Abbey

14. A Cornish stone-walled house from around AD 25

15. A reconstruction of a lake village dwelling

16. A hearth in a reconstructed lake village dwelling

St Anthony Head

The pictographs on the arch over the south door to the church of St Anthony-in-Roseland say that Jesus came with his uncle to Cornwall for tin. Their boat got into trouble where the St Anthony Lighthouse is today and where later a chapel was built dedicated to St Anne, Jesus' grandmother, who came from just across the waters, in Brittany. This chapel was built right out on the rocks in the sea, following the practice of those times of building small chapels to commemorate events. Centuries later, in 1835, the St Anthony Lighthouse was built on the foundations of this chapel. The sea levels have dropped since the time of Jesus and the lighthouse now stands on the headland. The story says that Joseph and Jesus with their boat and the crew became caught on the treacherous reefs off St Anthony Head. The traders brought Joseph's damaged boat into the bay at Place and while they were making it seaworthy they stayed there. As it was a trading post they had somewhere to stay and it was convenient also as being a principal place from which tin was exported. They left behind a shrine with an account of their visit on it, and the church is thought to have been established on top of this shrine some time afterwards.

St Just-in-Roseland

There is a tradition that Jesus also came to St Just, one version being that 'Joseph of Arimathea and our Lord came in a boat and anchored in St Just Creek.' When more traders' ships were present than could be safely beached at Place it is very likely that some would go to St Just where the creek also afforded a safe anchorage.

The informant of this tradition was a Rector of St Just-in-Roseland, the Revd J.V. Hammond, who told the Revd H.A. Lewis, the author of *Christ in Cornwall?*, that 'a number of older people still say that "Christ came to St Just."' The Revd H.A. Lewis tells of a man in Falmouth who, as a boy, spent much of his time at St Just and later used to visit the farmers in their homes when acting as a local preacher. This man recorded how he used to sit with the farmers on the beach below the church, waiting for the tide to bring barges of manure. Often as not, he said, the conversation would come round to the holy legend, and that, 'it was as much as your life was worth' to express any doubts about Christ coming to St Just.

Local people also used to point to a certain flat stone, with curious but unintelligible markings on it, which they said was 'the stone on which Christ stepped' when he landed. The present whereabouts of this stone are not known, but from the description given it could have been one of the votive stones to their sun-god that the Phoenicians set up in places to which they travelled. These stones usually had sun-crosses carved on them in various styles together with a series of cup circles, the circles having different meanings according to their number and position on the stone relative to other carvings. For example, two cup circles designated the resurrecting sun-god, three circles represented death and four circles the Mother. Votive stones dating from about 400 BC and carved with sun-crosses and accompanied by texts written in the Ogam script have been found in the upper Don valley in Aberdeenshire in Scotland, set up by Phoenician explorers as they travelled through the area. It is very probable that the stone with its markings that the local people found unintelligible and that once stood at St Just was a Phoenician votive stone to their sun-god.

The Scilly Isles

The Scilly Isles, also known as the Hesperides or the 'Blessed Isles', are mentioned in several early documents of the tin trade, where the islands are called the Cassiterides. The Merchants' Point on Tresco is said to be so named because the Phoenicians came there to barter for tin brought over from the mainland by the Britons.

Descriptions of the number of islands making up the Cassiterides vary between the ancient writers, probably because some of the islands were at different times uninhabited. According to Timaeus (c. 400 BC):

Opposite to Celtiberia are a number of islands, by the Greeks called Cassiterides in consequence of their abounding in tin, and facing the promontory of the Arrotrebae are the six islands of the gods, which some people have called 'the Fortunate Islands'.

Dionysius of Alexandria, a bishop and theologian of the third century, wrote concerning Cape Ortegal at the northernmost tip of Spain, near to Corunna:

> Against the sacred Cape,
> th'Hesperides along the ocean spread;
> whose wealthy hills with mines of tin abound,
> and stout Iberians till the fertile ground.

The Greek geographer Strabo wrote the following concerning the tin-traders, and appears to be describing a brotherhood living in the Scilly Isles:

> The Cassiterides are ten in number and lie near each other in the ocean towards the north from the haven of the Artabri [Corunna]. One of them is desert, but the others are inhabited by men in black cloaks, clad in tunics reaching to the feet, girt about the breast, and walking with staves, thus resembling the furies we see in tragic representations ... Of the metals, they have tin and lead which, with skins, they barter with the merchants for earthenware, salt and brazen metals.

5

Glastonbury

After visiting Cornwall to trade for tin, if he was to collect copper and lead Joseph's business would have required a journey to the area around the Mendip Hills in Somerset and to Glastonbury.

The Revd C.C. Dobson tells us, in *Did Our Lord visit Britain, as they say in Cornwall and Somerset?*, that there is a Somerset tradition that Joseph and Jesus 'came in a ship of Tarshish to the Summerland and sojourned in a place called Paradise'. The Summerland is taken to be Somerset. 'Tarshish' is derived from an old Semitic root found in Akkadian meaning to melt or to be smelted. A 'ship of Tarshish' thus probably refers to any vessel involved in the trade in metals, whether carrying ore or smelted metals. These were ocean-going vessels with a large sail and capable of being rowed in heavy seas. 'Tarshish' also sometimes refers to a place (the locality is much argued about by scholars), as in this passage by the prophet Ezekiel, writing in about 600 BC concerning the evident wealth of the Phoenicians as traders in metals: 'Tarshish was thy merchant by reason of the multitude of all kind of riches; with silver, iron, tin, and lead, they traded in thy fairs.' (Ezekiel, Chapter 27, verse 12.) The prophet Jonah, seeking

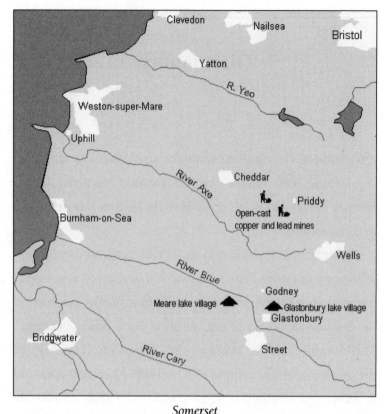

Somerset

to escape God's call, himself boarded a ship going to Tarshish and the account relates how the crew rowed hard in the fierce storm that ensued (Jonah, Chapter 1).

Following their visit to Cornwall to collect tin, Joseph and Jesus would have taken their 'ship of Tarshish' around the Cornish coast and moored near Burnham or Uphill in Somerset. On their way they might have called at the mouth of the Camel in Cornwall, where the estuary provides a large natural harbour, to collect fresh supplies, including water. On the bleak, windswept downs of St Minver to the north of the Camel estuary, where one would hardly expect to find fresh water, there is a well known as the 'Jesus Well'.

According to Thomas Quiller-Couch, who in the nineteenth century made a series of notes on ancient wells which were later published by his two daughters in *Ancient and Holy Wells of Cornwall*, above the well there once stood a building, 'square in form, with a highly pitched but truncated roof of masonry. A niche of rude shape is in the further end of the wall.' Quiller-Couch quotes from the *History of Trigg Minor*, whose author, John Maclean, wrote of a Jesus Chapel that stood near the well. He said that the building had a doorway with a two-centred arch consisting of three stones, but that 'it is now much out of repair'.

He wrote that the well possessed a fine spring, the waters of which were believed to have great healing properties, and that people came from long distances to use the waters. Today, the well and the building have both been repaired and stand within a small enclosure on the golf course north of the village of Rock. The well is signposted and there is a series of small white posts defining the track to the well.

Legend says that Joseph and Jesus rested on their journey at a place called 'Paradise', a name that appears on some old maps as the name for the area around Burnham. There was a Paradise House, a Paradise Farm and, until recently, a Paradise Hotel. Uphill on the coast north of Burnham is reputed to have once been a port used by the merchants of old. From here, Joseph and Jesus would have journeyed by river boat up the River Axe to Priddy, a small village lying at the top of the Mendips and the centre of what then was the copper and lead mining area and where there is an age-old proverb that runs, 'As sure as our Lord was at Priddy.'

An old folk song makes reference to Jesus going to Priddy:

O Joseph came a-sailing over the sea,
A-trading of metal, a-trading came he
And he made his way to Priddy
With our dear Lord.
O Joseph. Joseph!
Joseph was a tinner, was he.

O Joseph came a-sailing all over the sea,
A-bringing a turg of the holy thorn tree
From the bitter, cruel crown
Of our own dear Lord.
O Joseph. Joseph!
Joseph was a tinner, was he.

The Revd H.A. Lewis, in the second edition of his book, *Christ in Cornwall?*, recounts how a former schoolteacher in Priddy used to recall his pupils from their wandering thoughts to the lesson in hand with the admonition, 'Suppose you saw Jesus coming up the hill now?' — a memory, Lewis suggests, of an earlier time when Jesus 'walked up the long coulee from Nyland to the crest of the Mendips'.

From Priddy, Joseph and Jesus would have travelled by dug-out canoe through the marshes and along the River Brue, past Godney, which means God-marsh-island, and down to Glastonbury. The lowland area that now lies to the north and west of Glastonbury is not like it was 2000 years ago. Then, the River Brue flowed past Glastonbury Tor and turned north, not east as it does today, and drained into the River Axe. The flow of the River Brue was sluggish and the whole lowland area was a marsh, comprising a number of small pools of water with here and there some drier patches where birch and alder trees grew. To find a route through to Glastonbury would have required local knowledge, and Joseph would have probably engaged the services of someone to act as a pilot and guide to him and Jesus as they made their way through the waterlogged marshes.

Access to the lake village settlements was by boat. Log boats, cut from a single oak trunk, measuring in some cases over 20 feet long and capable of carrying loads weighing up to a ton, were the means by which the smelted lead and copper were conveyed to Joseph's ships moored at Uphill. An ancient log boat was discovered when the Glastonbury lake village was excavated and this boat is today preserved in the Glastonbury Museum.

Joseph and Jesus at Glastonbury

When Joseph of Arimathea first came to Glastonbury it would have been to trade for the copper and lead which were then obtained from open-cast mines (the remains of which can be seen today) at Priddy and from other nearby sources on the Mendips.

Archaeological excavations have revealed that iron and bronze were both worked at Glastonbury and in the other lake villages. Iron was not smelted on-site, due to the impossibility of achieving the high temperatures required, but was traded for in the form of bars that could be forged into tools. Joseph may have traded these sword-shaped 'cur-

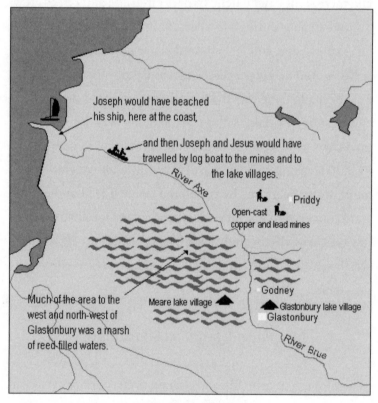

The Summerland

rency bars' of iron for copper and lead. Glass beads of a style suggesting that they were imported from the Continent were discovered when the Glastonbury lake village site was excavated. These, as well as amber beads from the Baltic, might have formed part of the lake villagers' trade for metals. Cordoned bowls from France have been discovered at a cave site at Wookey Hole. The trade in tin involved a journey through France from Brittany to the Mediterranean using pack-horses to carry the ingots, and bowls such as these might have been brought on the return journey to Britain.

Harness and bridle fittings have also been found, but because conditions in the lake villages would have been unsuitable for horses they were probably tethered there for short periods only. They might have been used for transporting lead from the mines at Priddy and elsewhere on the Mendips. The fine workmanship of the metal and bone harness fittings indicate that their owners were wealthy.

I will now address the question of what Jesus would have been doing while Joseph was busily occupied in trade at Glastonbury, and will introduce the part the Druids possibly played in Jesus' formative years.

The Druids

Some writers suggest that the primary reason that Jesus came to Britain was to meet with the Druids and to return to the earthly source of divine knowledge which the Druids appear to have inherited, at least in part. Their suggestion is that Jesus accompanied his uncle when he went to Glastonbury for a cargo of lead, found people there who thought as he did, and stayed for a time and studied in preparation for his ministry at the Druid university that was then at Glastonbury.

Myths, legends, fraudulent scholarship and deliberate fabrications all make it difficult to establish the truth concerning the Druids, whose traditions and teachings were only transmitted orally. It has been said that Gwyddon Ganhèbon, the Seth of the Book of Genesis and the third son of Adam and Eve, founded Druidism and that it was brought to Britain by Hu Gadarn, a contemporary of Abraham, under whose successors it became established as both the spiritual and the civil leadership of our island. In his book *St. Paul in Britain*, the Revd R.W. Morgan, drawing on an unknown source, wrote, 'There can be no question that this [the Druidic religion] was the primitive religion of mankind, covering at one period in various forms the whole surface of the ancient world.' The sources of Druidic theology are not always deemed to be sound. But I believe there is sufficient, reasonable evidence – which we will now examine – to support the theory that Jesus came to Glastonbury and resided there in order to study with the Druids.

The origin of the name 'Druid' is uncertain, but it might derive from *drui* or 'man of knowledge'. The Druid spoke with a voice that came from a deep spiritual consciousness, for he was the seer of all that was, all that had been, and all that was yet to come. There are things in common between the Druidic and Jewish teachings. The Druids were not polytheistic but believed in one invisible God and in the preexistence and immortality of the soul. They called this one invisible God, Du-W, meaning the one without any darkness, but believed that his real name was an ineffable mystery, as also was his real nature. They also believed in a Trinity, saying that God, to the human mind though not to himself, represented a triple aspect: Beli the Creator represented the past; Taran the preserver of providence in the present; and Yesu the Saviour who was to come in the future. Caesar wrote: 'The Druids teach that by no other way than the ransoming of man's life by the life of man is reconciliation with the divine justice of the immortal gods possible.' This shows that they had a doctrine of atonement as well as a Saviour, Yesu.

Here was a faith proclaiming the coming Christ under the name of Yesu and enshrining in its doctrine the principle of atonement. In these respects Druidism anticipated the coming of Christ and Christianity. We cannot say for certain that Jesus enrolled at the Druidic university at Glastonbury. It required 20 years to master the circle of Druidic knowledge of natural philosophy, astronomy, arithmetic, geometry, jurisprudence, medicine, poetry and oratory. But one should not wonder if Jesus did come to reside here in Britain. Western Britain at that time was unconquered by the Romans and remote from Roman influence and authority. Free from the Pharisaical misinterpretation of God's laws, in Druidic Britain Jesus could live and study among people who held the ideals that later he would proclaim in Palestine. It may be that the Druids agreed that Jesus could live and study for a time with them, having been impressed in the same manner as the teachers in the Temple at Jerusalem were astonished at the boy Jesus' learning when at the age of twelve he went to Jerusalem with his parents for the Passover. And Glastonbury would have been a more suitable place for quiet preparation for ministry than Galilee, which appears to have been known at that time as a breeding ground for sedition and lawlessness, as typified in the statement in the Gospels, 'Can anything good come out of Nazareth?'

There are parallels between Druidic teachings, the law of Moses and Jesus' teachings. When Jesus gave his message with a force of knowledge and learning that caused much wonder among the Jewish elders, it may have been due to his studying the revealed Mosaic law in conjunction with the oral secrets of Druidism. Druidism in Britain was a very moral, elevating and beneficent religion, offering 'the truth against the world', and not to be confused with the more pagan and sacrificial habits that occurred in Gaul, about which Caesar also wrote. 'To look lovingly upon the faces of little children', comes from a Druid triad of three things that all men should love, and corresponds to Jesus' teaching on the importance of being like children and of such being the kingdom of heaven.

Another parallel is seen in the extreme penalty invested in the Druids and the one most feared: that of excommunication and expulsion from both the present world and the future world. It is echoed in Jesus' teaching, found in the Gospel of Matthew, Chapter 12, verse 32, when he says that for whoever speaks against the Holy Spirit there will be no forgiveness, either in this age or in the age to come — still one of the most troubling passages for many Christians today.

After Christ had been crucified, when Joseph of Arimathea returned to Britain and Glastonbury to announce that the Saviour had come with a name familiar to every Druid, and had fulfilled the expected atonement, it is not surprising that his news was welcomed. Druidism never opposed Christianity and eventually became voluntarily merged with it. And in Britain an echo of the Druidic name for the coming Saviour, Yesu, still survives in the name Jesu, used in some of our ancient hymns.

Jesus' home at Glastonbury

In order to settle at Glastonbury for the purpose of study, Jesus would have needed somewhere to stay, and legend and later writings suggest that he built a home for himself there. The original building would probably have been a circular hut, constructed in the style of the Britons, made of clay and wattle and thatched. When Joseph of Arimathea later returned to Glastonbury he either enclosed this hut in a rectangular church constructed of wood, or he built a church on the hut's foundations for use as a private chapel for himself and his companions.

There are references to this early building. First, there is a remarkable statement in a letter written in 597 by St Augustine of Canterbury to Pope Gregory the Great in which he states:

> In the western confines of Britain there is a certain royal island of large extent, surrounded by water, abounding in all the beauties of nature and necessaries of life. In it the first neophites of Catholic law, God beforehand acquainting them, found a church constructed by no human art, but by the hands of Christ himself for the salvation of his people. The Almighty has made it manifest by many miracles and mysterious visitations that He continues to watch over it as sacred to Himself, and to Mary, the Mother of God.

The translation 'by the hands of Christ himself' comes from the book *St. Paul in Britain* by the Revd R.W. Morgan who is quoting from an early manuscript bearing the title *Epistolæ ad Gregoniam Papam*. In the ancient manuscript used by William of Malmesbury the Latin expression is *a Deo paratam*, which translates, 'by God Himself':

> Now there was a certain royal island within the confines of the realm [of Athelstan], called in the old language of the vicinity Glastonia ... consecrated by the gifts of God

Himself. Indeed, when they came into these parts, the first neophites of the Catholic law, under the guidance of God, found a church constructed (as they say) by no human art, but actually prepared by God Himself [*a Deo paratam*] for the salvation of man.

There is another and certainly older (*c.* AD 1000) manuscript by an anonymous Saxon priest writing on the life of St Dunstan, who has the phrase *coelitus paratam*, that is, 'divinely constructed', and where the sceptical words *ut ferunt* ('as they say') were either omitted or only in the margin. Whichever version is preferred, it is a material building that is being referred to, that the builder of the church is Christ himself, and that God, 'the Almighty', watches over it.

Augustine arrived in Britain in AD 597, probably expecting to find the whole island pagan. The eastern part of the country which the Saxons had invaded and where they had settled was undoubtedly pagan. But Augustine found in the western parts, into which the Britons had retreated, a British church. The island in the 'western confines of Britain' to which he refers is no doubt Glastonbury, and whoever the 'first neophites of Catholic law' were, whether they were the returning Joseph of Arimathea and his companions or some others, they clearly found standing there a church building that was said to have been erected by divine hands. William of Malmesbury actually saw the old church. Writing in the twelfth century in *Acts of the Kings of Britain*, he records that such was the reverence Augustine accorded to 'the Ealde Chirche' at Glastonbury, as it was known in Saxon times, that his companion, Paulinus, covered the church with a protective covering of boards to preserve it.

A significant statement also appeared in some folios of the Domesday Book, compiled in AD 1086, which refers to this house of God as 'the Secret of the Lord' and reads as follows:

> The Domus Dei, in the great Monastery of Glastinbury, called the Secret of the Lord. This Glastinbury church possesses in its own Villa XII hides of land which have never paid tax.

The Revd R.W. Morgan, who gives both the original Latin and the reference in the Domesday Book folio, takes this quotation from *St. Paul in Britain*. The same quotation, but from a different folio, appears in a work by Archbishop Usher entitled, *Britannicarum Ecclesiarum Antiquitates*.

These manuscripts point to Jesus having built a house for himself to serve as a home during a protracted stay at Glastonbury. At the time when Jesus would have been constructing his house on the uplands of Glastonbury on the Druidic university campus, the waters to the north and west of Glastonbury were rising and threatening the lake villages. The lake villagers were losing the battle against the encroaching waters and their villages and homes were breaking up. Perhaps Jesus had this in mind in his Sermon on the Mount expressed in the Gospel of Matthew, when in

Chapter 7 and beginning at verse 24 he spoke about two men, one building on rock and the other on sand, and the effect of the rising waters on each house resulting in the house built on rock standing and the house built on sand crashing down.

6

Jesus in the Villages

The settlements in Cornwall

On the Land's End peninsula there are the remains of about 40 Celtic courtyard-house villages. These clustered settlements came into being at around AD 25, probably about the time when Jesus was still in Britain. Each settlement comprised a number of oval, stone-walled houses in which the rooms opened out onto a central courtyard. A fine example is found at Porthmeor, with another good example at Chysauster, the best known of these villages, where eight houses lie on either side of a street with their backs against the south-west wind. In each dwelling there is a workshop, a living room and a stable, while outside there is a small garden plot. The remains of small villages are found on the moors of Bodmin, Dartmoor and West Penwith, close to where tin was streamed. On Bodmin Moor there are also the remains of villages where communities lived in groups of round, stone-walled huts with their roofs raftered and thatched.

The earliest people working tin probably worked part of their time as tin workers and the remaining time as farmers. The people living in these village communities might have met Jesus through working tin for Joseph. If they heard and accepted his teachings it may well be that the first people living what might be described as a New Testament life lived in villages in Britain and not in Palestine.

The lake villages of Somerset

In Somerset, the moors leading west from Glastonbury today are not as they were during the time when Joseph and Jesus would have come here. The entire area was a marsh of reed-filled waters, with a few drier patches where birch and alder trees grew thickly, bounded by a vast raised bog of moss, cotton-grass and heather.

Some time around 250 BC, a small group of people made their way through the marshes that lay to the west and north-west of the Glastonbury uplands to an area where slightly drier conditions prevailed and here they established a village. They began by dumping a pile of brushwood, bracken and rushes on the wet marsh, followed by layers of alder and oak logs or thick branches placed criss-cross on top. Upon this was spread a covering of clay, and the whole formed a base for the village and its open-air areas, shelters and round houses.

A barricade was constructed around parts of the village to stabilize the foundations. It was made of lines of alder posts driven into the soft peat of the marsh and these posts supported a woven wattle fence of about one metre high. The clay, which with the timbers formed the base and flooring of the village, was held in place by the barricade which also helped to protect the site from spreading and breaking apart.

The houses were made by first driving posts into the clay to form a circle. These posts were then linked by rods woven together or with woven panels tied to the posts and the whole was packed with clay, inside and out, to make a strong and windproof wall. The roof was thatched with reed, straw or heather, tied in bundles and fixed to the rafters. In the centre of the house was a hearth. Outside were small sheds, barns and pens for animals. Wooden walkways provided pathways within the village and to the outside. Because these settlements were surrounded by water this created a need for small boats that could provide easy access to the villages. So there was also a causeway or landing stage for boats and to provide an area for laying out fishing nets for drying or repair.

At Glastonbury there was a lake village, rediscovered in 1892, while to the west there lay a raised bog of moss, cotton-grass and heather that undulated and stretched westwards towards Meare, where other smaller lake villages had been established and which were rediscovered from 1895 onwards. Items found during the excavations of the Glastonbury lake village have shown that this was a busy and prosperous village and one of the richest Iron Age settlements in Britain. In one house a very large, rectangular hearth was discovered, decorated with 67 circles incised into its surface.

It is thought that it was actually a table rather than a hearth. This stone with its incised circles is reminiscent of the Phoenician flat votive stones and speaks further of the relationship of the inhabitants of the lake villages with the traders of metals.

It is, perhaps, inaccurate to describe these as lake villages, given that the village at Glastonbury was built on a marsh and those at Meare on the edge of the raised bog. None was actually a village in a lake, but the name 'lake villages' has entered into common parlance. Why there was a separation of people at Glastonbury into those who dwelt in the lake villages and those on the upland area where the town of Glastonbury stands today is not clear. It may be that the upland area was reserved as the campus for the Druidic university there. What does seem probable is that Jesus knew and mingled with both populations.

The British historian Gildas (AD 516–70), wrote in his *De Excidio*:

> Despite the coldness of the climate and the distance of these islands from the natural sun, Christ, the True Son, afforded his light, the knowledge of his precepts, to our island during the height of [*tempore summo*] the reign of Tiberias Caesar.

Gildas' statement *tempore summo* has been disputed. It has been translated as 'last year of', but 'height of' seems the most probable translation because Tiberias Caesar died in AD 37.

The height of the reign of Tiberias Caesar would be from about AD 20–27, before he retired to Caprae.

In view of St Augustine's words in his letter to Pope Gregory,

> ...found a Church constructed by no human art but by the hands of Christ himself...

it may well be taken literally that Christ himself taught

> ...the knowledge of his precepts,

This view gains added force when we remember that Gildas spent the closing years of his life at Glastonbury.

Further evidence that Jesus taught the people in the lake villages during his stay at Glastonbury comes from the words of the bard Taliesin, who said,

> Christ, the word from the beginning, was from the beginning our Teacher, and we never lost his teaching.

This staggering statement reveals a continuity of Christianity, beginning with Christ himself and coming forward to our present day. It began when Jesus lived in Britain.

A road sign in Lostwithiel

Bibliography

Dobson, The Revd C.C., *Did Our Lord visit Britain, as they say in Cornwall and Somerset?* Avalon Press, Glastonbury 1936

Gildas, *The Ruin of Britain, and other works*, edited and translated by Michael Winterbottom, Phillimore, London 1978

Harte, Edward, *The Story of Place St. Anthony in Roseland, Truro, Cornwall: a souvenir booklet*, Oscar Blackford, Truro [1965]

Le Braz, Anatole, *Au Pays des Pardons*, Calmann-Levy, Paris 1925

Lewis, The Revd H.A., *The Child Christ at Lammana*, 1934, reprinted from the *Cornish Times* (copy in the Cornish Studies Centre, Redruth)

— *'Ab Antiquo'. The Story of Lammana, Looe Island, etc.*, 1935, reprinted from the *Cornish Times* (copy in the Cornish Studies Centre, Redruth)

— *Christ in Cornwall?*, Lake & Co., Falmouth 1939; 2nd edition W.H. Smith & Son, Glastonbury 1946

Lewis, The Revd Lionel, *St. Joseph of Arimathea at Glastonbury*, Avalon Press, Glastonbury; A.R. Mowbray, London, Oxford 1922; 7th edition, James Clark & Co., London 1955

MacLean, John, *Parochial and Family History of the Deanery of Trigg Minor, in the County of Cornwall*, Nichols & Sons, London, Bodmin 1872–9

Morgan, The Revd R.W., *St. Paul in Britain*, London 1861

Naraya, R.K., *Mahabharata*, Penguin Modern Classics, London 2001

Quiller-Couch, M. and L., *Ancient and Holy Wells of Cornwall*, Chas. J. Clark, London 1894

Strachan, Gordon, *Jesus the Master Builder*, Floris Books, Edinburgh 1998

Waddell, L.A., *The Phoenician Origin of Britons, Scots and Anglo-Saxons*, Williams & Norgate, 1924; The Christian Book Club of America, 1983; facsimile of 1st (1924) edition, Banton 1990

Wilson, H.H., *The Vishnu Purana*, a translation, Trübner, London 1864; facsimile of 1864 edition published by Garland, New York, London 1981